Yorkshire Coast & Moors
PANORAMAS

JOHN POTTER

MYRIAD
LONDON

CONTENTS

YORKSHIRE COAST   4

NORTH YORK MOORS   60

YORKSHIRE COAST

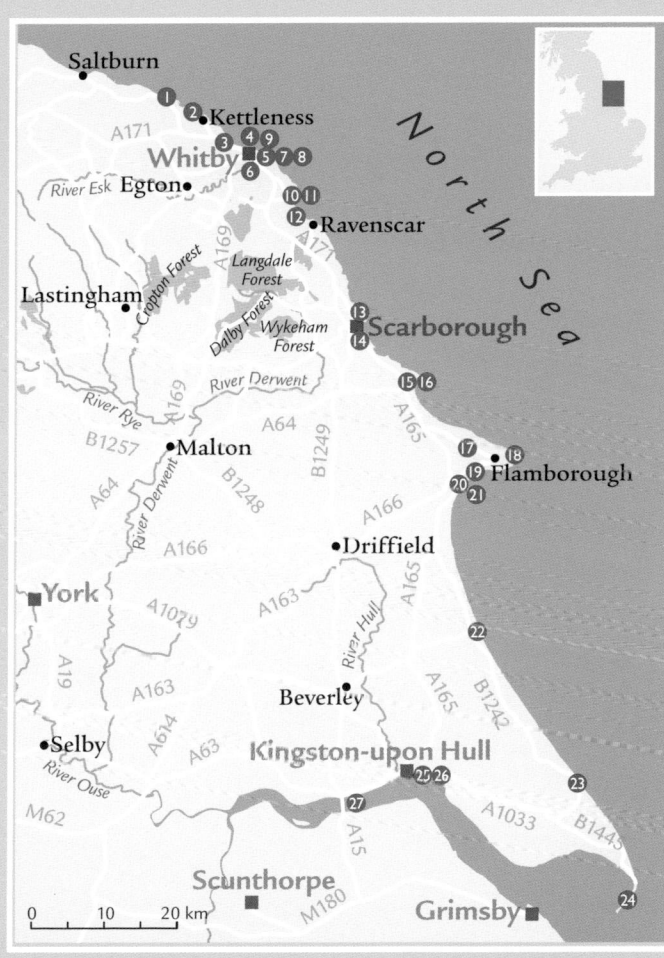

1	STAITHES	6
2	RUNSWICK BAY	8
3	SANDSEND	10
4	WHITBY HARBOUR	12
5	WEST PIER, WHITBY	14
6	WHITBY, OLD TOWN	16
7	SALTWICK BAY	18
8	SALTWICK BAY BIRDS	20
9	BLACK NAB	22
10	ROBIN HOOD'S BAY	24
11	BAY NESS	26
12	STOUP BROW TRAIL	28
13	SCARBOROUGH HARBOUR	30
14	SCARBOROUGH CASTLE & OLD TOWN	32
15	FILEY	34
16	FILEY BRIGG	36
17	BEMPTON GANNETS	38
18	THORNWICK BAY	40
19	SEWERBY HALL	42
20	BRIDLINGTON	44
21	BRIDLINGTON HARBOUR	46
22	HORNSEA	48
23	WITHERNSEA	50
24	SPURN POINT	52
25	HULL MARINA	54
26	THE DEEP	56
27	HUMBER BRIDGE	58

The spectacular Yorkshire coast stretches from the county border at Staithes to Spurn Point on the northern banks of the Humber estuary. The North Yorkshire Heritage Coast forms the seaward edge of the North York Moors National Park. This is a rugged and dramatic coast of high cliffs, punctuated by bays and wooded "wykes", traditional unspoilt fishing villages, river inlets, and wide sandy bays topped with majestic headlands. The larger fishing ports of Whitby, Scarborough, Bridlington and Hull are steeped in history and charm, drawing holidaymakers, artists, photographers and poets to this stunningly beautiful region.

OPPOSITE – THORNWICK BAY
One of Flamborough Head's many rocky coves

STAITHES

Looking from the harbour at low tide in late summer the dramatic and picturesque setting of this delightful fishing village is breathtaking. Staithes is known colloquially as "Steers" meaning "landing place" and oozes character and charm, having "snickleways" and alleys, galleries and craft shops, tea rooms and fishermen's cottages all haphazardly perched on any available space. The narrow road down into the village is so steep that visitors are advised to leave their cars in the clifftop car park.

RUNSWICK BAY

ICK BAY

Situated at the foot of steep cliffs between Staithes and Sandsend, Runswick Bay has a unique and glorious setting. This sheltered bay, with its long sandy beach, provided safe anchorage for fishing boats for centuries before it became a favourite of artists and then holidaymakers. The village, seen here from the boat park full of cobles (small wooden fishing boats) is a mass of narrow winding alleys and paths that weave their way between dozens of pretty cottages with their lovingly tended gardens.

SANDSEND

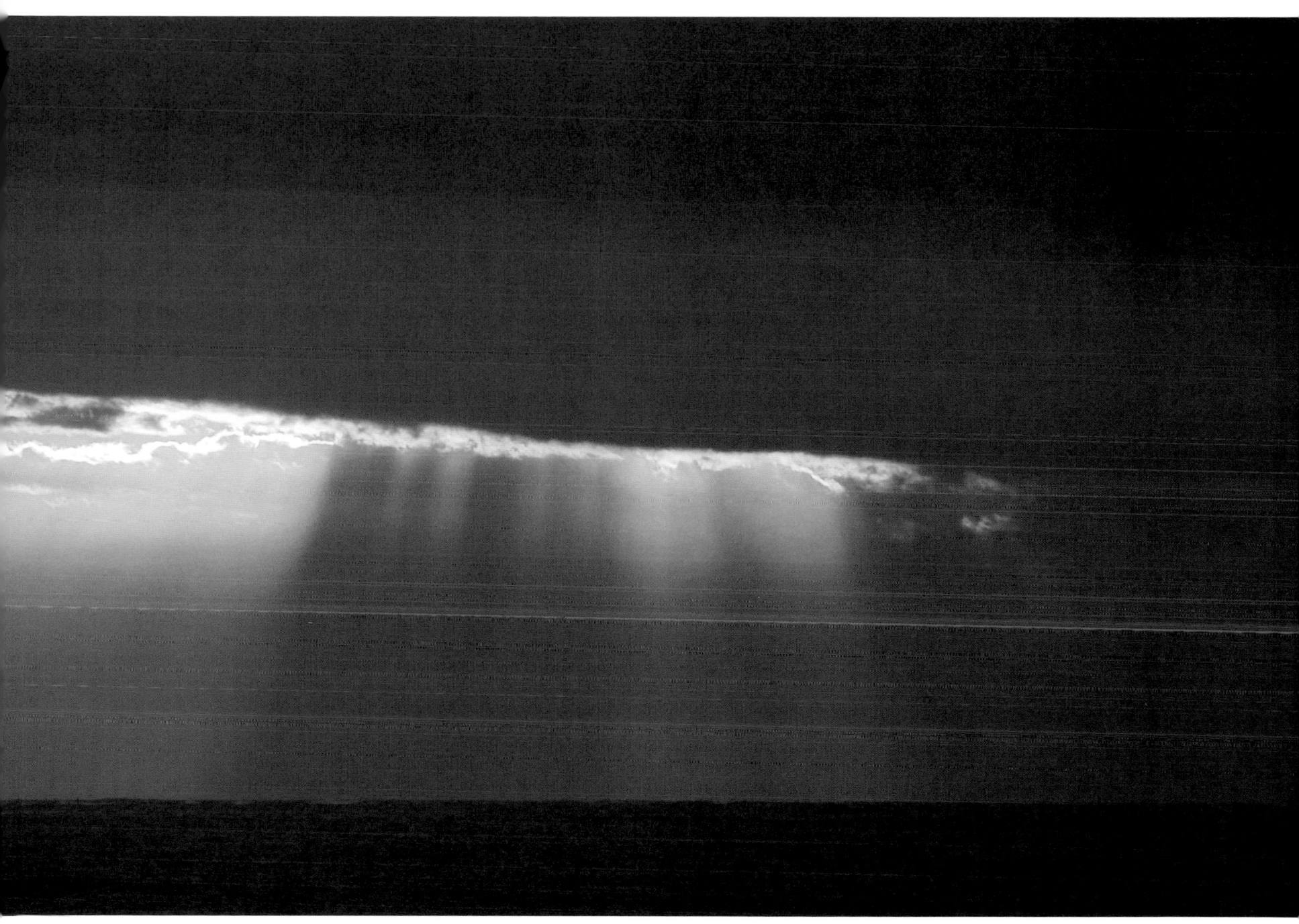

These distant cliffs just north of Sandsend, seen from the the pier at Whitby, stand proud at the foot of Lythe Bank. This spectacular location was once the site of the Saltburn to Whitby railway line. The old railway trackbed now provides walkers with wonderful sea views together with an eerie landscape of spoil heaps, a relic of the textile and tanning industries of centuries past. Just inland from the village are the remains of Mulgrave Castle, hidden away deep within Mulgrave Woods.

WHITBY HARBOUR

Often referred to as "Captain Cook's Country", the attractive seaside town of Whitby is where the young James Cook learned the seafaring trade. This view of the pre-sunrise glow on a cold and windy winter morning was taken from the West Pier where the ruins of the beautiful 13th century St Hilda's Abbey can be seen at the top of the East Cliff behind the Old Town. The nearby church of St Mary is one of the finest Anglo-Saxon churches in the north of England.

WEST PIER, WHITBY

The West Pier at Whitby is a real magnet for photographers and artists as it forms such a dramatic and stunning feature in the landscape. This is a hardy band of people who will often rise well before dawn and travel dozens of miles to set up cameras or easels in time for a spectacular sunrise. The weathered boards of the pier, the lighthouse in the middle distance and the rows of elegant Victorian hotels on the West Cliff are all a source of inspiration.

WHITBY, OLD TOWN

This view of the East Cliff has to be one of the finest vistas along the Yorkshire coast. The best time to see it is just as warm sunshine begins to bathe the front of the many quaint cottages and buildings that make up the Old Town, when the picturesque scene takes on a wonderful almost three-dimensional character. Local photographer Frank Meadow Sutcliffe (1853-1941) immortalised the town and the life of its maritime community in exquisite, sepia-toned photographs, many of which can be seen at the Sutcliffe Gallery in the new town.

SALTWICK BAY

The stretch of coast between Whitby and Scarborough is littered with archaeological remains and shipwrecks. Here at Saltwick Bay, just one mile south of Whitby, lies the remains of HMHS *Rohilla*, a hospital ship of 7,114 tons which belonged to the British India Steam Navigation Company. The ship smashed into a reef near Saltwick Nab on October 30 1914 and 62 crew and 28 passengers were lost. This picturesque bay is popular with surfers and fossil-hunters.

SALTWICK BAY BIRDS

If you venture down into Saltwick Bay at first light, well before the caravaners at the cliff-top site have stirred, you may catch sight of large flocks of seabirds. With their black and white plumage and bright orange bills, oystercatchers create a stunning spectacle when in flight. They can usually only be photographed from some distance, since the birds are particularly sensitive to any human presence.

BLACK NAB

The North Yorkshire coastline has numerous high cliffs, rocky coves and sandy bays where rock formations are exposed and easily seen, though not always easily reached. Black Nab is a very well-known local landmark, and is easy to reach when the tide is low, but visitors should take care to check on the times of the incoming tide which can sweep in at high speed.

ROBIN HOOD'S BAY

Taken in mid-August, this panoramic view of Robin Hood's Bay from Beacon Hows, just inland from Ravenscar, marks the place where the heather-clad moorland reaches the North Sea. The area between Robin Hood's Bay and Ravenscar has several wonderful footpaths, including the long-distance footpath, the Cleveland Way, which offers glorious uninterrupted views out to sea. This ancient standing stone provides the perfect foreground focal point, set amidst colourful heather.

BAY NESS

Robin Hood's Bay, with its narrow streets and quaint cottages, nestles in a ravine at the edge of a wide sweeping bay. This view from the cairn on Stoup Brow Trail shows sea fret – a very common occurrence on the east coast – lingering above Bay Ness, the headland to the north of the village. The Coast to Coast long-distance footpath which starts at St Bees in Cumbria ends at Robin Hood's Bay and exhausted walkers are often seen paddling their tired feet at the shallow water's edge.

STOUP BROW TRAIL

The Stoup Brow Trail hugs the cliffs above Ravenscar, which is often referred to as "the town that never was". It was the failed brainchild of the Ravenscar Estate Company who, in 1895, bought the entire area for £10,000 with the intention of creating a brand new seaside resort to challenge the established nearby towns of Whitby and Scarborough. Perched at a height of 600ft (183m), the Raven Hall Hotel is just visible on the skyline above the cliffs which soar to 400ft (122m) above sea level.

SCARBOROUGH HARBOUR

Scarborough was Britain's first seaside resort, and is one of England's most popular coastal towns. Founded just over 1,000 years ago, Scarborough is, historically, a relatively young settlement. Its name is derived from that of Thorgils Skarthi, a Viking raider who settled on this rocky and wild headland. The harbour consists of three piers which enclose an outer and inner harbour. The outer is used mainly for pleasure boats and the inner (pictured here) for fishing and passenger vessels.

32   SCARBOROUGH CASTLE & OLD TOWN

This view of the inner harbour around mid-morning in September is from the balcony of the fishermen's café on the south pier, which has a splendid view of the harbour, town and castle. The castle defends a prominent headland between two bays with sheer drops to the sea. It was subject to repeated sieges in the Middle Ages and during the Civil War and was damaged by naval bombardment in the First World War.

FILEY

The elegant seaside resort of Filey is blessed with five glorious miles of sandy beach protected from the north by Filey Brigg, a promontory which juts out 5,200ft (1600m) into the sea. At low tide the Brigg is a haven for fishermen, naturalists, artists and fossil-hunters. Running out from the Brigg is a mysterious rock structure which is thought to be the remains of an ancient harbour, which may have served the Roman signal station of around 395AD situated on the cliffs above.

FILEY BRIGG

The warm sunshine of an early autumn sunrise bathes the rocks on Filey Brigg at low tide. The Brigg is a reef of calcareous grit, which has provided shelter for ships and seafarers over the centuries. Until the mid-19th century the village of Filey consisted of a small seafaring community gathered around the present Queen Street. Today visitors to this attractive resort can enjoy the sight of jaunty fishing boats at rest on "the cobbles", the landing stage which forms part of the beach.

BEMPTON GANNETS

At 400ft (122m), Bempton has some of the highest cliffs on the east coast of Britain and is one of the most important seabird nature reserves on the east coast. The gannet colony – the largest on the UK mainland – can be seen from the clifftop at Bempton between January and November but is most active between April and August during the breeding season. Access to the reserve is relatively easy either by car or on foot from the little village of Bempton, just one mile inland.

THORNWICK BAY

The magnificent coastline around Flamborough Head combines stunning white cliffs with picturesque sheltered shingle coves fronting the sea. Jutting out miles into the North Sea, this headland was declared a Heritage Coast site in 1979. These special areas of protected coastline are managed so that their natural beauty and wildlife are conserved and, where possible, access for the public is improved.

SEWERBY HALL

Sewerby village is a small hamlet on the coast just two miles north of Bridlington. Sewerby Hall, on the edge of the village, is set in 50 acres of landscaped gardens and is a Grade I listed building. The house was built between 1714 and 1720 by John Greame and the rooms on the ground floor are in a mix of Georgian, Regency and Victorian styles. The park and gardens include a zoo, woodland walks, formal and walled gardens (above) and picnic areas.

BRIDLINGTON

Bridlington is located to the south of Flamborough Head. The town is divided into two parts: the historic market town, approximately one mile inland, which developed around the abbey of Bridlington Priory and the fishing port of Bridlington Quay, which developed as a holiday resort in Victorian times with the arrival of the railway in 1846. Today Bridlington is a lively town with a picturesque harbour and two glorious sandy beaches.

BRIDLINGTON HARBOUR

Fishing boats, sailing boats, pleasure boats and speedboats are moored side by side in this attractive and historic harbour. Bridlington is still a busy fishing port, and fishermen land their catch every day to sell either from their boats or at local markets. Bridlington is the home of the official museum of the East Riding of Yorkshire, which is housed at Sewerby Hall. In centuries past Bridlington was situated two miles inland and the town only expanded out to the coast when tourism developed in the late 19th century.

HORNSEA

Hornsea is a small and very popular seaside resort situated 16 miles north of Hull. The heart of the town is a conservation area with some houses dating back to the 15th century. The resort is fringed with attractive pebble and sandy beaches and has a newly developed promenade. From the seafront there are spectacular views southwards towards Spurn Head and the entrance to the Humber estuary. The beach lies at the eastern end of the Trans-Pennine Trail which finishes at Southport in Lancashire.

WITHERNSEA

Withernsea developed as a holiday resort around a much smaller settlement after the railway was built to connect it with Hull in 1854. In 1875 a concrete sea wall and an ornamental iron pier were constructed by the Withernsea Improvement Company. Tragically the pier was seriously damaged in 1880 by the coal barge *Saffron* and then in 1882 swept away by a ferocious storm. The ornamental castellated pier towers still remain as an entrance to the beach.

SPURN POINT

Spurn Point, situated on the north bank of the entrance to the river Humber, is an important feeding and stopping-off point for thousands of migrating birds. The three-mile long finger of land that arcs out into the Humber estuary is constantly being reshaped by storms and coastal erosion. The distinctive black-and-white Spurn lighthouse became redundant in 1985 and has been replaced by automatic beacons.

HULL MARINA

The Humber and Railway Dock in the centre of Hull was once at the heart of a large complex which housed the city's whaling and deep-sea fishing fleets. Now the dock is part of the Hull Marina, constructed in 1983. The distinctive black vessel is the old Spurn Lightship which was previously moored east of Spurn Point. Built in 1927, the ship has been restored and guided tours are available.

THE DEEP

The Deep, the gleaming glass and aluminium marine life centre, opened in 2002. Designed by architect Sir Terry Farrell, it stands at the confluence of the rivers Hull and Humber and is part of the vision of regeneration for the city of Hull. The Deep houses one of the most spectacular aquariums in the world, and is home to 40 sharks and over 3,500 fish. Behind the scenes a dedicated team of marine biologists cares for the animals and carries out vital research into the marine environment.

HUMBER BRIDGE

The Humber Bridge was designed and built to cross the last major estuary without a bridge in Britain. It links north Lincolnshire to the south with the East Riding of Yorkshire. The north tower of this amazing structure is sited on the high-water line and the south tower founded in shallow water 1,650ft (500m) from the shore. Construction began in 1973 and the bridge opened in 1981. The new road link cut 50 miles off the journey between the ports of Hull and Grimsby.

NORTH YORK MOORS

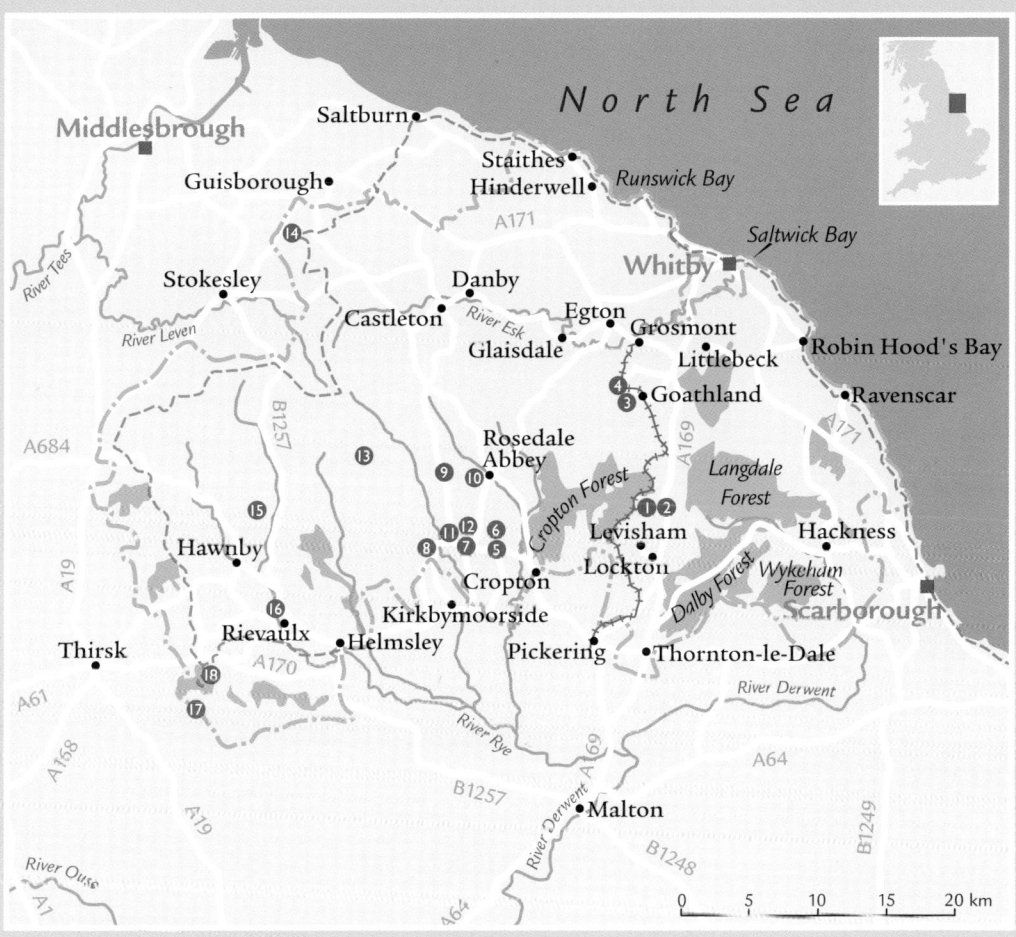

1	THE HOLE OF HORCUM	62
2	DESERTED FARM, LOW HORCUM	64
3	MALLYAN SPOUT	66
4	BECK HOLE	68
5	LASTINGHAM	70
6	LASTINGHAM MOOR	72
7	HUTTON-LE-HOLE	74
8	SURPRISE VIEW	76
9	BLAKEY RIDGE	78
10	ROSEDALE	80
11	FARNDALE IN AUTUMN	82
12	FARNDALE IN SPRING	84
13	BRANSDALE	86
14	ROSEBERRY TOPPING	88
15	BILSDALE	90
16	RIEVAULX ABBEY	92
17	WHITE HORSE OF KILBURN	94
18	SUTTON BANK	96

The North York Moors provide a varied and spectacular rural landscape, combining vast expanses of purple heather-clad moorland, farming dales and extensive woodlands. The area is dotted with medieval castles, abbeys and pretty villages as well as many relics of a bygone industrial age. The national park is bounded to the east by the North Yorkshire Heritage Coast and in the west by the Hambleton and Cleveland Hills. The author James Herriot described the breathtaking view from Sutton Bank on the western fringes of the region as "the finest in England".

OPPOSITE – SHEEP AT GOATHLAND

This beautiful village, high in the Esk valley, has been the setting for many television programmes and films

THE HOLE OF HORCUM

The Hole of Horcum is a large, crater-like amphitheatre carved out of the valley of Levisham Beck, just north of Levisham and Lockton, between Pickering and Goathland. Legend has it that this glacial feature, nicknamed the "Devil's Punchbowl", was created by the devil when he scooped the earth out of the valley bottom and tossed it to one side. The three hills of Blakey Topping, Freeborough Hill and Roseberry Topping are supposedly the result of the earth being thrown across the moors.

DESERTED FARM, LOW HORCUM

The Hole of Horcum is a popular spot for sightseeing trips. This natural amphitheatre is easily accessible from the main Pickering to Whitby road which runs
alongside the heather-clad moor. A splendid walk from the roadside car park goes down through the centre of the basin and on to the pretty villages of Lockton and Levisham.
The walk passes by this derelict farm cottage at Low Horcum.

MALLYAN SPOUT

Goathland is a favourite with visitors who come to take a ride on a steam train on the North Yorkshire Moors Railway or walk around the village made famous as "Aidensfield" in the popular television series *Heartbeat*. Mallyan Spout, the highest waterfall on the North York Moors, is close to the Mallyan Spout Hotel at the western edge of the village. It tumbles 60ft (18m) down the deep and beautiful West Beck Gorge.

68

BECK HOLE

Beck Hole is located at the northern fringes of the ancient Great Forest of Pickering and is one of Yorkshire's best-known villages. It has a truly tranquil setting, hidden away at the bottom of a small wooded valley close to the river Esk. This picturesque hamlet can be reached from Goathland along a single track road. The settlement consists of only nine cottages, two farms and the Birch Hall Inn close to the bridge.

LASTINGHAM

Lastingham holds a unique place in the hearts of Christians who have been visiting this site for centuries. At the behest of St Cedd monks from Lindisfarne built a monastery here in 655. Sadly the monastery was destroyed but Abbot Stephen of Whitby built a crypt to replace it in 1078 in which the saint's bones were interred. The crypt can be seen in the church of St Mary in the village. Directly opposite is The Blacksmiths Arms inn.

LASTINGHAM MOOR

Looking across Lastingham Moor, the tower and roof of the church of St Mary in Lastingham village are just visible amongst the trees. Throughout the centuries, this was the view which thousands of pilgrims crossing the moor had of their final destination – the tomb of St Cedd housed in the crypt under the church. This early Christian saint from Lindisfarne died of the plague in 664, shortly after attending the great Christian gathering – the Synod of Whitby.

HUTTON-LE-HOLE

One of the most popular stopping-off points for visitors to the North York Moors, Hutton's broad village green is best-known and loved for its moorland sheep which wander freely grazing on the grass and searching for titbits left by holidaymakers. The village is home to the Ryedale Folk Museum, the region's leading open-air museum which has three acres of displays depicting life on the Moors through the centuries.

SURPRISE VIEW

Gillamoor is a pretty village nestling at the southern end of Farndale – often known as the "Daffodil Dale" due to the swathes of these attractive flowers which adorn the local hedgerows and cover the river banks in spring. This panoramic or "surprise view" can be seen at the eastern edge of the village close to St Aidan's church as the minor road swings sharp left and down the hill towards Hutton-Le-Hole and Farndale.

BLAKEY RIDGE

Blakey Ridge above Farndale and Rosedale is peppered with Bronze Age burial mounds and standing stones. A section of the Coast to Coast Walk traverses Blakey Ridge, from Clay Bank to Grosmont, following the line of these Bronze Age relics. This dramatic standing stone is located near the main road that links Hutton Le Hole to Castleton. The remote 16th century Lion Inn, sited at the highest point of the North York Moors National Park, is an ideal gathering point for walkers.

ROSEDALE

This view of Rosedale from Blakey Ridge was photographed just north of the Lion Inn very early on a bitterly cold winter morning. Access along the Castleton road in midwinter can be tricky and it is not uncommon for the road to be blocked by drifting snow. The beautiful Rosedale valley is approximately eight miles long and here at the head of the valley there are traces of old mineworkings and a disused railway track that is now used as a pathway for ramblers.

FARNDALE IN AUTUMN

Taken from the slopes of Round Crag, just below Blakey Ridge, this photograph looking west towards Potter's Nab just above Head House Farm captures the vibrant autumn colours of Farndale in October. The golden drifts of bracken and the yellows of the foliage contrast beautifully with the rich vibrant greens of the fields across the valley. In the past bracken was gathered in the autumn for animal bedding, fertiliser (in ash form) and horticultural use.

FARNDALE IN SPRING

This view is from Daleside Road at the foot of Horn Ridge looking towards the tiny and picturesque hamlet of Church Houses in the middle distance. This remote hamlet nestles between the mighty Rudland Rigg and Blakey Ridge amidst stunning scenery at the very heart of this much-loved dale. Farndale attracts around 40,000 visitors each April who come to walk along the banks of the river Dove amongst the wild daffodils.

BRANSDALE

Situated between Farndale and Bilsdale, running north to south and stretching for approximately seven miles north of Helmsley, Bransdale is one of the North York Moors' best-kept secrets. In spring, the south-facing woodland photographed here is carpeted with bluebells. On Hodge Beck in the valley bottom is Bransdale Mill, a refurbished water mill owned by the National Trust, which is an overnight stop for school and conservation groups.

ROSEBERRY TOPPING

"When Roseberry Topping wears a cap, Let Cleveland then beware of a clap."

The distinctive conical-shaped summit of Roseberry Topping lies close to Great Ayton on the northern edge of the national park. The hill's peculiar shape is due to the fact that half the summit has collapsed, either because of geological faults or the many old alum and ironstone mines close to the top. As the old saying (left) indicates, Roseberry has long been used as a sign of impending bad weather by farmers and sailors.

BILSDALE

This magnificent view looks west over Bilsdale close to the B1257 Helmsley to Stokesley road about two miles north of Rievaulx Abbey. Here it is possible to look across the valley of the river Seph towards Hawnby and Bilsdale West Moor, which reaches 1,293ft (394m). In the background is the distinctive brown mass of Cow Ridge, which forms the south-western edge of the Cleveland Hills.

RIVEAULX ABBEY

This 12th century abbey, now in ruins, was the first of eight major Cistercian houses in Yorkshire, and is arguably one of the finest monastic churches in northern Britain. It sits in a secluded location in a deep wooded valley just two miles north of Helmsley. Under Abbot Aelred (1147-67) Rievaulx prospered to such an extent that the abbey became over-crowded. From this elevated position it is clear how close local cottages are clustered to the enormous building.

WHITE HORSE OF KILBURN

SUTTON BANK

The view looking from Sutton Bank towards Roulston Scar and Hood Hill on the western edge of the North York Moors is one of the finest panoramas in northern Britain. Prevailing weather systems blowing eastwards across the Vale of York often create amazingly dramatic skies which create ever-changing vistas. In the distance, gliders can often be seen being towed skywards from the edge of Roulston Scar, the home of the Yorkshire Gliding Club.

Published in 2011 by Myriad Books Limited
35 Bishopsthorpe Road, London SE26 4PA

Photographs copyright © John Potter
Text copyright © John Potter

Designed by Jerry Goldie Graphic Design
Map artwork Stephen Dew

Printed in China

www.myriadbooks.com

ISBN 1 84746 135 2
EAN 978 1 84746 135 3

Kilburn's fame is linked to animals both large and small. This famous landmark is a huge figure cut into the hillside of Sutton Bank overlooking the village which can be seen from up to thirty miles away across the Vale of York. Kilburn was also the home of the woodworker Robert Thompson, the "Mouseman of Kilburn", a craftsman known for his carved mouse trademark found on church pews throughout north Yorkshire.